AUTOMATON BIOGRAPHIES

AUTOMATON
BIOGRAPHIES

Larissa Lai

Arsenal Pulp Press
Vancouver

AUTOMATON BIOGRAPHIES
Copyright © 2009 by Larissa Lai

SECOND PRINTING: 2015

ARSENAL PULP PRESS
Suite 202–211 East Georgia Street
Vancouver, BC
Canada V6A 1Z6
arsenalpulp.com

The publisher gratefully acknowledges the support of the Canada Council for
the Arts and the British Columbia Arts Council for its publishing program, and
the Government of Canada through the Book Publishing Industry Develop-
ment Program and the Government of British Columbia through the Book
Publishing Tax Credit Program for its publishing activities.

Cover illustration by Keith Langergraber
Book design by Shyla Seller

Printed and bound in Canada on FSC-certified paper

Library and Archives Canada Cataloguing in Publication

Lai, Larissa, 1967-
          Automaton biographies / Larissa Lai.
Poems.
ISBN 978-1-55152-292-0

          I. Title.

PS8573.A3775A87 2009   C811'.54   C2009-903749-1

four eyes

contents

rachel

It is not clear who makes and who is made in the relation between human and machine. It is not clear what is mind and what is body in machines that resolve into coding practices ... There is no fundamental, ontological separation in our formal knowledge of machine and organism, of technical and organic. The replicant Rachel in the Ridley Scott film Blade Runner stands as the image of cyborg culture's fear, love, and confusion.

—Donna Haraway, "A Cyborg Manifesto"

Look, it's me with my mother.

—Rachel, Blade Runner

•

2019 and all's well
i tower my mythic birth
my father's a doll maker
his algorithms spill life
more human than human   → mora Heat
                           than Hevt:
                           techno-Orientalism

i dream an ethic
pure as lieder
pale as north
moth before industrialization

we manage our doric columns
even the sun
the way light tumbles
through our boardroom
rues our mumbly owl

light gold flecks our eyes flutter
wisdom of inward sisters

.

a chilly mortal
but mortal still
i'm all business
here to demonstrate perfection

my father's enterprise
rations my emotional response time
pupil is the empty space
through which light passes

my retina imprint
such photosensitive paper

[handwritten margin note:] robotic
perples
perple-
like robots

.

i camp policeman
testing cold because the accident
nothing really wrong
he hides what he can't bear

i well against his
emotional calfskins
his killing jar
his girlie magazine's
gooey centre

•

i half my memory
what's past is polaroid

i collect water in ditches
my body ticks out
its even rhythm too flawless
for birth

i athena my own sprouting
this knowledge colds me
in my ice-fringed room
my asian fits this frost

i owl my blink
slow stare i thought was mine
father given

my heart exudes a kind of love
a kind of mourning

only policemen recognize me
with any heat

i dream insect hatching
my brother's incest
curious as logic
of folded paper

i hang memory on icy lines
tedious laundry
someone else's dirt

i pride my fear
i clutch my hate
my soft youth
dolls plastic as capital want → post-industrialist post-capitalist

i marvel my limbs' articulation
warmth my heart makes from nothing
for no one but the hand
that winds me

·

this rage i told you
i toy my own mind
quick computation brings ugly feelings
terror the old man
is not my father
is god in his heaven
and what's right with the world?

．

phantom police station reorients
city of angels
dystopic rain
kabuki's coca-cola billboards

tug this fur collar
against my plastic face
her memories or mine?

my heart's an egg timer
spilling sand
gravity goes on forever

pretty policeman's seen the letter
the law of my birth
four years line my fibre
his rib? or any other part
belonging to a man

i search my memory's lineage
for signs of suture
a kiss is just a sigh
a scar
lipping the star of midwife

*Rachel here
knows her
background,
nature, being*

•

this secret thread and tendril
he knows
this intimate doctor
sailor, policeman, chief

i auto every memory
mimetic someone else's
dead mother spider
someone else's curious brother

policeman's hands are hot
as tears my ducts
manufacture this dribble
i salt   i water

·

he noirs his murders
long coat big gun
a kiss is just a bullet wound
he knows my innermost
femming this fatal injury

.

they said the blood spatter
was extraordinary
an aesthetically pleasing
splash of red against
clear cellophane coat
they said her pale skin glistened
under pink and blue neon
and a million shards of broken glass
they said there was a glimmer of pain in his eyes

he flashed his
i.d. like a hero

exotic of the Orient // exotic of the cyborgian

.

chinatown's best snake dancer
exotic limbs
art of face

the future we sight still
in shot wounds
foreign coil
wrings dystopia
from others we mark <u>contagious</u>
by sound by eye

shattered language
tonal and broken
a playground to backdrop
our slippage

we mechanize communal
anxious as trenchcoats
drinking to excess
after a bad killing

.

i'm not lost
it's the city

under assembly-line eyes
fresh as new bruises
that is, dilapidated ancient
nothing's new under the gun

olympia curses vision
spin about, wooden doll

my eyes fine as china
man could make them

mr sandman send me a scream
eyes burn
for a gouging

first time i saw my own kind
large on street
it was leon
shaggy head not noble
but proud

he'd have killed my policeman
in less than twenty questions
crushed him
like an origami dog

my policeman, i said
is this love?

into the back of leon's skull
my gun pumps the answer

.

now our fates tie us
my murderer and i

he shams state sanction
says no choice
spits blood
aches like something
made of meat

pain is a sign of guilt
knows my skin and leon's
cede serial and cellular
from the same code

.

i see double
roy told him
if only you could see
what i've seen with your eyes

mine slant half-bred
i foe my love
law fascinates
its big guns grieve

policeman drinks
knows my joker's goggles
seat something like a soul

i'm unhinged unsteady
street shimmers absence
presence doubled over

my balance is off
not inner ear
but "i" say
if in agreement
"aye"

my favour
not mine to give
you threaten
i repeat
your desire

like Orient reflects Decident

i'm inflatable
sex doll requires mouth
to animate

pull the plug
i sigh hiss
leave for the death
which is not one

can not sustain my
insubstantial flesh
without plastic
covering of consent

i float ghostly
a hot air incubus
made of breath and want

.

this melancholy pisses me off
i rank my anger
rail against this solitude
was a princess with perfect clothes
beloved daughter of a new elysium
our flawless manufacture
had shed earth's dirt
imperfection's disease toil filth

i super my human's bright
privilege my exemplary
perfection exquisite as orbit

i race my swagger
contagion feminine

the sub-altern

my excellence flickers
gasps for gas
a small blue flame
suddenly cut

•

we peace the too pale too blond
super in ur-forest's fresh breeze
its limpid lakes and crystal rivers

our century jades terror
knowledge my athena
wars for us
the blunt rapes
the mass racial graves

fear is the proper mode of living today (pandemic method sorry)

i mourn purity
in guilt in fear
my perfect construction's
the instrument of

·

only photographs
will stave the terror
look, it's me with my mother

this sensitive surface
scarred by light

o my beloved replication
dual and singing
our wind-up beauty shatters
without witness

missed event lingers
at faded edges

i shove my proof
beneath his derisive nose
someone else's, he says

but i know when i'm gone
he presses to his chest
the picture of the ancestor
who looks like me

replicant at large
my dangerous twin
skirting the shoulder of orion

angel on fire
different devil's descent
your doll's clothes flail
in false light's breeze

you tumble
a hailstorm of brilliant candy
duplicit as idealistic missiles
gushing atomic rain

.

related by blood
kindred in kind
perfection is our flaw

our racial differences mechanic
eyes limbs secret
parts design-soaked
and calculated in advance

superior strength
minds sharp as
haystack needles
unpredictable and algorithmic   *ironic* ←
death is our only weakness

we hinge mortal on mortality
post our mortems on other wings
judeo-christian logic pumps our hope
for a graceful ascent

after all that sky-high living
not in heaven
but some place like it

our father which art
artful we tender girls
love what our supreme boys
would kill for

34

between misplaced love and violent rage
we abject our elsewheres
shining bright as warrior constellations
we came down from

.

in her dilapidated carnival palace
my deadly double
barnums her daily seductions
on cartesian logic

our degenerate kin
marvel with wide eyes
and liars' noses

does she understand
our father's fascist dream?

she handles hot eggs
menaces our genetics
her feminine charms our longing

we know we're not innocent
her abject masks
a painted face

this automatic bride
among other sad girl
manikins waiting too long
in white

•

deckard finds her quickly
his senses six our other digits
uncanny prescience

the murderer in me
loves the murderer in you

my quick twin
handsprings a wailing weapon
lupine howls clench thighs

play to win
ride the skull
crack walnuts
sweet as christmas soldiers

•

couldn't kill her
because of me
my lover's lover's alibi
differences blood in this
deadly circus

her eyes and mine
grown from the same sad stare

our hair sprouts from the same source
our flesh pours from the same vat

o bone of my bone
confused and parched by longing
when did you know what you were?
when did you choose
a lover like yourself?

i went to the other side
false identification
internalized racism
loving the alien
clothed as the same

what does a woman want?
i doll my rage this original
apple too hot for my small hands

its red burns me

faith in wiring
we illegitimate offspring
our father's lawful
monsters to turn or not to turn

like Frankenstein & monster

we dream our broken
reproductions online
we repeat
on department store shelves

post-industrialist

give me a battery
my wires heat on semiconductor technology
my microprocessor accelerates
rate of exchange
heightens military levels of alert

foreign threat hinges
my soft body
disposable
down to the last cell

Pandemic as Method

.

gotcha, deckard
we dream the same dream
gaff's seen your impossible
beast folds this delicate
paper knowledge

your human
subject's broken star
our crossed wires clutch ever bigger
guns they hold
our "i"
this certainty

too bad she won't live
but then, who does?
death bottle
corks this fountain
our elevators seal breath
moment's crumpled aware

all along
you were one of us

dear mother

0111001001100101011101000111010101110010011011100001000
0001110100011011111001000000011011000110000101101110001 10
0111011110101011010010111001101101000 that is to say 0110000
10110111001100111011101010110100101110011011010100000100
0000110111101100110001000000011001100110111101110011 0010011
0010101101001011001110110111100110010101110010100100100
1110011001000000011001100110111110110010001100100011 0010
101110010 otherwise 01110100011010000110010100100000 0110
0010011011110110000101110010011001000110010101110010 01000
10000001110000011010010110001101110100011101010111001
0011001010111001 1 a mixture of 01100011011000010110111001
100001011001000110000100100000011101110110100101 1011 00
01100100001000000110010101101110011011110110101011001
1101101000001000000111010001101111001000000111001001 10
0101011101000111001001100001011000110110101100100000001
1100100110000101101001011011000111011101100001011 11001
cn to cnn and rpms to dna 0111010001101000011001010010000 0
11000100110010101101110011001000010000001101001011 01110
0010000001101101011110010010000001100011011011110111001
00110111001100100101110010

love rachel

nascent fashion

•

case stated in white and white
nation born off a boat
all contention and emergent
clauses our ambulances
claim soggy sailors
slow separations

we dream tomorrow's murders
in dolby sound surround
advance guards tickets
stages side show
for sad dancers
simian simulations

we dot our lines
bloody signatures
traces name our children
tumble to other lineages
we forget our own

．

sing of stunned classrooms
beg scientific truth
off bureaucratic buck
buy long-distance packages
want the untouchable beloved's
wireless futures
derivative of tomorrows
already sold

our brutal histories hang
on glossy string
railroads and internments buffed
attract the foreign current

keep the cash
deter the bodies
corridor power buzzes fresh
bleach and lemon

we zap our tongues
on the satellite dish

·

UN contemplates retaliation
stars wrap artefacts
biblical past black marketed
reinterpret to fundamental future
flag unfurls liquid
assets and other oil

we fluid until the body
until stripes teenage gentle uniforms
dumbstruck civilize the birth place

we barbarian our projection
worship the misinterpretation
book the innocent
to redress

hands can't see
the blood that covers them

•

the pilots who refused
miraculous vision through heat
memory stretches
civilians crawl market still
bodied stretches
to where i wasn't

what i remember
other planes other bombs
the hot flesh that peeled
daily chatter sip coffee
klatch cake jam old warmths
your rope back before
even if disturbed by blond dreams
ur-forests even if disturbed

rome twin
engined even if
attila the hundred the inquisition
monarchic intrigues the murder
the burnings conquest the americas
trade slave the a-bomb reduction of place to death

tail-spin the plummet
a split remembering

member back when
peace man
frag men and fragile as
soft
and almost legal frog men
self-contained
and underwater breathing
back when rapid eye meant
dreaming the movement
rev the solution not pieces
the whole engine engine number nine
no money-back guarantee
no tender equal

only limbs and eyes
and scattered sear the shard the shrapnel
the peace we promise
to keep materiel personal
and flowing off assembly
no right to unless it lines

come unto these metal hands
and there ignite the right
on sister her fury all human tissue

i spirit because the frag
the pea the princess felt it all
and who could sleep
for all the explosions

.

exposure unknown
agent arms open
and blazing
germ in the machine

o my lovely double
elsewhere and shining
fear the manoeuvre
my biochemical package
the secret mitosis of girls
nights thick with hot paste

ancient thrall of anthrax my old
acquaintance forgot at the mere touch
down and downier
hard copy broad and helmeted
sweet winged nike
dashes for the long needle

the anecdote
to save the grand narrative

•

it is dark and she
it is dark so thirsty and the smell
my body their bodies all this rot
this shit this vomit this blood

i didn't know i wanted
wanted the white bed
was that so bad?
white bed all crisp cotton and down
high posts a girl
i could yell at

i'd make her pay make her
anger i didn't see
the mirror myself ghost
white bed for ghost girl
wanted to help my parents
wanted a girl to rage at

this girl
is dark and she
so thirsty the smell
hunger long gone
air cries crises gap

in dark my body their bodies
old scarfaced bag who yells
at me i'll make her pay

the factory girl who pinches
the girl who cries who pricks her finger
who strains her eyes
the girl with chemical burns
the girl who suffocated
the girl with the severed hand

the girl i want
not this dark

the white bed in the glossy
advertisement i saw and the white
girl in the white dress so pure
i wanted
not this ghost

a girl to do
what i say

not me

am i a girl dreaming i'm in a truck
or a truck dreaming i contain a girl?

.

all containers are dark inside
whatever engine
its oily ancient fuel
whatever medium
asphalt salt water fresh water track

i thorn my foot to escape the shoe
dim the lights myself
before the boss does
who is a man
what is a machine
what has a mind
what is web-enabled

o parent
corporation my body
a cell to be bought
i flash appear when you need me
based in turkey
shanghaied to vietnam
former yugoslavs slave as
mexican labourers max hours
push borders that pushed back
illegal where once master
carded now home without

uniform my black hair
flesh rip each time the contract
relocates the girl
the same girl different

my dreams rust containers
i slow boat from china
to meet yesterday's demand

.

emergency rings on the dollar
calls planes to existence
immanent and breathing
we pass as pigeons

ideological contagion stools
digital signals and flags
wave hands semaphoric
call for metaphor the fundamental
whine of discontent

we civil our eyes as towers
twin the geography of a thousand and one
brown elsewheres we marked as target
market labour pool

disposable as plastic razors
double action blade for a cool smooth
sexy until the bluff
the snuff cleanly
executed in real time imovie

the biochemical bludgeon
half-lives deplete cancerous uranium
military aircraft flatten desperate
breed of suicide

we mime our own grief
for vérité of hourly cast
spell horror at flash recognition
we share soft biology

difference our capacity for hardware
our impermeable fear
we factor in our right to win

this sorrow in the innocent
part the longing
imperialism's imperative scathes
we dirt even in revolution

desire awry
we force we blood we maim
she body she collective

in our innocent we search
culture's purgative rhetoric
as machines repetitive wilt spirit
as bones dig mass racial graves

our soft that works tears burns
dismembered and bleeding
she dark she poor
this litany all tongue-stuck and word-full
innocent digs for itself

absolute abstract
calls to body's miraculous
pulse and warm this soft
reproduces kisses even the hindered
belly blossoms

pretend a fresh garden
sing the charred cell's
delectable mutation phantom
pleasure of severed limb

chant the cancer regenerative
our brilliant pustules recall brine
of origin the new salt
futures a city of soft

biological meteors replicate
scale our feather our alien
innocent all damp and downy

.

already used i know
already held up and heralded i know
child the one god
our hate hot divine
thin slip of goodevil
double's godly devilry

i cave my truck hate
i anger my own blood
the girl outside in
i long i fury i spit so acid

the floor burns

•

1931 to 2003 manchuria remembers its comfort
we woman our stations conflict
convention centres denial
meat red and sensitive to sharp

393 western syndicated news sources
spring at this racial
regloss reread those yellow bodies
they savage they horde the unknowable
quantify flesh in pounds per square inch

the pressure we human
all righteous in our west nest

they atrocity they guilt
and we read
our heart rates at the thought

we dare their sick
our eager coin in small print back pages
while she daughter she mother she auntie she child
front this desire for the white bed

or this desperate this bored
machinic rhythm of terror's hunger
hammers flesh like metal
and calls it love

·

my opera's optimum topia:
scholar's daughter's modest courtyard
terrace all breezy warm
south china sees no opium
our masses earth religion
heaven wafts incense smoke

soldiers in smart form
fruit juicy families or
lounge their bodies firm
pleasure by consent

the other clock's time
ticks on warm sand
our glass holds yellow light

i book apsaras off cave walls
sing sores closing
guns wilt in children's hands
arms inspect presidents for rhetoric of mass deception

bombs drop cherry orchards
blossom pink kisses and champagne
lost boys pass poetic license
in fundamental churches

punishment's present
returns repressed desire in ribboned boxes
spilling fresh mud finger paint melted chocolate
lolls soft bodies slippery and glowing

sweatshops evaporate in heat shimmer
release trapped dreams to parched land
labour's liquid longing sprouts proletarian palaces
grapes and pomegranates tumble
into calloused hands
as pesticides turn to silver glitter
and incense dust
makes everyone beautiful and kissy
without ulterior motive

future stretches on brilliant city
all multiple and shattered and singing

left the opium and myopia outside
my dark truck that stifles
that moves me risking borders
and prison in the name of protection

i truck my love
i hate my truck
i web my dreaming's sticky silk
to wear this fine weaving

i strong my solitude but
it wells my anger i told you
not nice my teeth sharpen in darkness

i gene my fury in this shit stink
theirs my own
piss this rank anger
these insect bitches
forced entry to bloodstream
the man who leers and rubs

dangles future business
as possibility of possibility
demo mocked by rapid privilege
of cash flow

·

in the dark is a country
this neo geo all re-nation and proud
we ideal we protect we value we human
inside this stink dark
my moist rage

don't know which country
matter the road
which project laboured
which taxes
which pride our rapid transit
moves necessary packaging
arbitrary content
leaves labour power raw

this rational economy begs transportation
to unlimit consumption
flows commodities in wastes out
on pipe on wheel on rail by air
my air i choke this moving dark
standardize container
to maximize swap of mode

dark the same
country the same
i right my reverse
machine my equivalent
bed my white want
all lace and threadcount

diaphanous curtains billow
in video's rank breeze

•

big ghosts contra
band my diction war
korea's north sees red as
america flags china's chopped limb

british crowns hong kong
cut for duplicity more capitalist than capitalist
trades commie goods
slant contagion

door slam hello hunger
remember japan's occupation
desperate flee inland seeking
kuomintang line as red gushes sweet at first
from north only to double back
in broken glass kneeling

we flay ourselves in dismay
headless corpses fragrance harbour
grandfather costumes jewellery chains debt
as father uncles scramble door to door
against america's abandonment

we dream superior technology
car camera oven
made of butter cookie tin

we joy our small
we praise america
envision a new europe

boots mark us red
double your labour
double the gun
teeth out of mother
tongue all lip left
on body ghosting english

i subject curse court curt discourse
hi normal yeah yeah sure boss
whatever you say

．

body's repetitions mark modern woman
my eye's eye
straining to acid scratch microchip
so fine my corridors
dexterous etching

retinal labour my shift's gaze
through scope
minute enlarges
hours lengthen
days dim 'til night brings
equality of vision
sight fades faces of family
beloved retreats to other arms

metal and angry
i touch to know
my labour's incapacity
as hands spasm
already contained
contain me again

i doll my series
smaller and more enclosed with each collapse
towards stifled kernel
crooked fingers
coiled spring tight and full of rage

·

automaton dreams sightless lovers
maiden form from midden heap
cog gear apple dry leaf mildew
negative map of masculine longing
as tongues catch empty
eye sockets and severed hands
scamper free of corporate hole

i language my body to being
ontology's on-switch
tender as rubber nipple
my skin flushes
flesh full as any cyborg

i arm my machine love
swing from limbo to limbo
right up the river
my amazon lethal as yellow mud

breathe my golly
my salem sailor's
supernumerary tipple and
unheimlich familiar

witchy witchy woman
american as gene genie
i replicate my sweet helix
doubled and coiling
you've come a long way baby

.

lost in lingo of limbo
i lycan my throat
shape L and R to tone loss
light rapid larceny

i bay my moon
docks desolate even
in cult of multi

read as terror divers
plunge the underling
to sub
strata alternates
a neatly striated pattern along
ridge of spine

we pressurize our breathing apparatus
internal cavities adapt
denser air

i breathe the long languish
dependent on regulator
as tongue tanks oxygen's
repressed knowledge
of joong sunk to drowned girl's
slang hanging off big country

my wolf's subaltern
adaptation to lung's collapse
and re-inflation as market speculates
lingua franca's latest orientation

·

we entered the desert in despair
guns blazing our hardware
out in the open

there could be no mistake
of our good intentions

we wore our hearts like soldiers
our sleeves flapped
in the dry wind

we lay our aggression
naked as we could
it was the only offering
we thought the desert would understand

we entered the desert
we thought it was empty

later we understood the strangers
we killed were like us
only different

the desert's emptiness
sparked our deepest dismay
we felt helpless in the face
of so much collateral damage

we thought we would never leave the desert
we thought we would always be alone
we offered our greatest sympathy
to one another

we thought the strangers
we had killed
were our brothers and sisters

we sought revenge

·

demonic mnemonic
memory repeats
shell of abandoned girl
flushed fleshy to recall
the want not want shift
of this kiss that stirs

tumble into the crash
the break that can't
recollect pieces pulpy as
organisms indeterminate life
unsure of entry and sharp
as shrapnel

harmonic hysteric mystic as
eleusis lucidly remembers
future descent into death

forgetful father's rail of corpses
open wounds protruding bones
that litter occupied streets
bedrooms of houses turned in by children
shattered girls left in stairwells

our good attempts to patch to hide
under a fine layer of leaves
forget to tell the girl

kisses are the plumb line to horror
the first word is silent soft
this coaxing call to loss

we girls who understand
dress as boys our armour
hard thick our tongues that cut
raw inside layered under
repeats insistent litany

desire as tomorrow's memory
ghosting visits our soft mouths wait for

·

empire dons freedom
as terms evacuate threads
demon in democracy ditches
goddess for refrigerator factory

dollars barrel up guns
weapons miss allusion
mask delusion's massive protrusion
misinformed in tight uniform
duke's micro nukes
intention to reheat war's cold leftovers

nike states of a meritless
longing to re-empty
the pyre already romanced
by earlier nations' stakes
in stocks locks and bonds
burning the querulous inquisitive
as which inquisition's with or against

heresy parsed and paraphrased
tongue forks freedom's vacant carcass
unstable cradles its innocent and
martyrs multiply in fear's daily ditches

.

holy whores ears open to pitch
fork trining tinpot tines

dictator evacuates meaning's lost cities
to gander's improper usage
demonstration plagues mother's
warriors goosed by the bump
in lumpen

proles profit in righteous rhetoric
guns law urban alleys
prisons complex farmscapes
off freeways' on-ramps

plant nation's gain of chains
gangs war uniforms and battle crises
recall totalizes termination
to populist pimple pop
parole for holy rollers and rich
sauces crag our jennytwenty

and other fast fixes
only the ones
our psychosexual credit can
one eight hundred

.

potions portioned consumes our magical
relations of reduction
west flesh presses constraints
we woman our portia's portal
say that you love me
christian this romance leapt to
imagining perfect arms

mark stretches to marked men
al-rashid's hotel bags rockets
launched on american technology

our heroes hinge
responsible occupation while
a thousand and one journalists
share their sad amble
to make plans for post-war iraq
was to signal our intention to go in
with or without the UN

secrets forge duplicitous code
under chivalric discourse
scout's honour dissipates
to intrigue against nights of gunfire

our sea change to exchange
languishes first use
american occupation
evacuates factory for tank

·

mockery in democracy laughs up
kuan yin's long flowing sleeve
we export what our floridas can
agent orange

ballot brother's swan song
to barnum brothers' three-ring binder
trapeze artists dazzle
grim clowns' skyward glance
game cannibalism against irreconcilable grief

we paint our glum faces
polka dot our regulation
gear our unicycles to count down
from zero

our sweet elephants
trumpet ankle chains
nozzle spray homesick tigers
against strong man's strong arm
of law stretched for the deep pocketed

in our floppy smocks we mock
our goose to the simulacra circus
hand out empty shells like candy
our souls balance high wire
taps as dancers ta ra ra ra boom de ay
to anthems emptied

all flags hallmark our sentimental journeys
to exotic elsewheres
we long range the rage
we can't admit against dark bodies
we can't extinguish

merchant of venus
spares roses for lost tires

late night highways without ama
we signal our delight in time's hiccup
this momentary reign of pink petals

bodied affection of lost goddesses
barefoot wandering along the dotted line

we travelled without signing
our roads salted warm enough
to spring dandelions through asphalt cracks

we ditch our furies to hiatus grim divisions
our sores sprout music and soft lighting

we boy our girls tender hands
to dance these haunted roads

time's momentary pocket of nothing
in the middle of nowhere

•

my destiny's not a nation
i covet cloth
swathing of good citizens
drapery that tugged roads roman leading

america the dutiful
bolt fabric's long roll
to stitch liberty's desert camouflage

their cocky green misunderstanding
my fundamental duality
i love you i hate you
daisy chains my weedy uncertainty

poisoned well irritates
roots to sprout legs like
ginseng man the dark forest's

hot incubus shoots out of earth
to walk to truck to haunt
these night routes

in the hollow parts
of anything that moves

.

on her majesty's secret surface
folds old skin
cell's degenerate memory
empire is as empire does

multinational operatives slip their lease
as lists plant names of face cards
joker trumps
deuces wild about ba'ath party's
most wanted

we spade
our clubs of mass detention
detective noirs
a kiss is just a kiss
we judas our guantanamo's ancient longing

clues accumulate to be ignored
war rages while cause evaporates
we street our puppets
bully proof vests
against all the vietnams in the world

ham

Having the same organ placement and internal suspension as man, plus a long medical research background, the chimpanzee chosen to ride the Redstone and perform a lever-pulling chore throughout the mission should not only test out the life-support system but prove that levers could be pulled during launch, weightlessness, and re-entry.

—Loyd S. Swenson Jr., James M. Grimwood, Charles C. Alexander, *This New Ocean: A History of Project Mercury*

I miss the earth so much
I miss my wife

—Elton John, "Rocket Man"

song

bang bang
chop chop chang

up in a rocket
what a man

culture 1, nature 1: rocket man

mimicry's flattery
           aping an ape
simian similar strikes familiar pose
                egging your difference
                            but not begging your pardon
                            the hard-on brought on by a queer fear
                                        i play monkey
                                                to your chicken

c1, n2: brother

                                                  i was there first

onwards and upwards
       all ambition   my nutrition's an addition
           to straightjacket neck-ring shock restraint
i'm tainted   almost human but not white
           98.5 percent checks out for biomedical verisimilitude
     human or animal
                       blights rights

      i hear muzak of spheres
            double planets' mud and gas
       my angels undulate   prehensile tails
your future the power of my now   emperor of the final frontier
     my space   ya dig?

c1, n3: darwin

                                              prior's prior
              the beauty of before
nostalgia howls   survival of the thickest
              my galapagos swims all manner of individual difference
pushing species diversity to mutate the future
              what you know about finches
                    you know about primates
                          what you know about primates
                                you know about
                                      you know who

c1, n4: noah

      in the desert
i saw my father's shame
            i told my brothers   sold the pun's fun
a lark for the mark
      of ham not cain
blame game precipitates guilt economy
        astronomy places stars crossing my southern horn
master's cold shoulder enslaves or indentures
innocent generations to mechanical motion
        human checked in middle passage
           nantes to neverland
land of the cree   home of depraved

c1, n5: jocasta

let me count the ways

                                                      i know my mother
                         genus of oedipus
                 complex nexus returns to bend gender's garden
rough labourer sex selects as culture
                       nurtures incestuous reversals
poor canaan it wasn't his fault
                 courting family curses and purses
                 if i could do it all over again

ditty

oops i did it again
      repetition's such a drag

c u later, not applicable: chinaman's hat

chop chop
                    right quick
          chop house chop stick chopped liver
                    chapsticks' slapstick
          me speakee   you freaky
mr sandman

                              pork chop   chopped ham
                    roast lamb   a can of spam
whenever you want me
all i have to do
                    is preen

c2, n2: koko-san

sign fine animal gorilla
        talk to the hand or put your foot in it
the same river twice   rolls dice   i'm the one who looks happy
hamming for the camera
       me cheetah   you jane
goodall could see the fear in my beer
nasa lackeys misreading my teeth

                    Un bel dì, vedremo
                    levarsi un fil di fumo
                    sull' estremo confin del mare

come again, sailor
i get paler all the time

97

c2, n3: mimicry

a cracked bone a slack dome
michelangelo refeats islamic technology
          sycophant in the bedroom
          recasts individual genius
a lie   you got it from a bottle
          coca-cola adds strife

c2, n4: monsanto's mutations

the gods must be lazy   books hazy after all that burning
       she taught me the dangers of organized religion
              stool pigeon   set up by the get up
and round-up ready for the word made flesh
        machine   dream of a common language
scribbled on ribosomes   dribbled in soma
       chroma of a butterfly wing
dreaming it's an arm
        racing for space
                       not the ham they think i am at home
                       i'm a rocket man

rondo

burning out the ruse of capital circulation
accumulation's second ticks in offshore banks
swifter than tankers can shift hard currency
digital dials
reaching out to touch someone

crime, punishment: nasa to coulston

major tom   submits to surgeon general
        an eye for an eye   a heart for a heart
xenobiotics exotic   calling same!   (different, so different)
        immunology's golly from ham to ham   that is
pig to chimp   limp on the inside
                          xenotransplanted in the name of love

c3, p2: first infection

porcine endogenous retrovirus   squirted by perverted science
        calling for cured meat   the duty of prosciutto
loved ones saved
      by the rave   and mad
                    manufacturing generic kidneys
                     intercellular labour
     machine in meat
cure for a broken heart   is another heart
        porcine docile   ham for compassion
    bacon for bacon
god-given dominion over animal   processes
      pathetic prosthetic someone else's real deal

c3, p3: cordelia

dry-cure my meat   loves salt
      no peer but the leer of the chimp's pimp
mission controls organ arrangement
                registers levers
shock of memory of shock   while earthbound spock babies
routinized on tested formula
     the blame and not white
sequence levers' proper timing
            the master's clock shall not destroy
            the master's rocket

c3, p4: deep inside we're all the same

or wet-cure in the brine of no time
                        flesh preserved in immunology's stolen hour
power of flowers cast to roadside while the whole hog goes on
        factory farming for meat or medicine
                    perv infects human cells in culture
vulture's nature to capitalize whatever moves   voracious
as polysexual possibility   viral's undiscriminating spiral
        too fluid to graph
                        or trace
           lace of our intimate biology
connected by the meekness of micro
                  the cycle that segues human to non

dance

a monkey or a pawn
      strength chesses in chains
                diagonal sidestep
a little cha cha cha
      with mother's other
                not man but ham

or nam our chop chop
      too close to airlift home

cure, curé: the tower

enki's genki   azimuth of flight path
          takes babel to shore
                    nam shub set for replication
language infectious and hot to trot
          anticipates weightlessness and galloping g's of descent
                              metal's heavy
                    repent before you push the button
scatter pattern of simian syllables
                              over atlantic   breaking up
ooo eee ah ah ah

c4, c2: paradise cost

gees of dissent
expectation's better brother

                                        bitten apple of capital
                                        happens on my map

        clap clap of elsewhere
        bitter grapple with western consumption
my body's cellular colonies
test our collective to represent

                                      interspecies jump
                              flu   spanish or bird

        herd flutters foreign
                    risk shock declines fish stock

c4, c3: looking out for number one

or the atlantic plunge
this is uncle tom to ground control
       group   the scoop on my 56 punch liver biopsies
                 liver marrow transplant and inoculation with HIV
i rock
              myself to sleep
                   bite my thumb   off the joint
there's no ointment for this appointment
           no prescription for the test case scenario

lament

to see difference   against strangeness of same
      species barrier porous at the level of marrow
      harrows blood
           brood i'm forbidden
               breeding experimental subjects
                   to research interspecies disease
    fleas i'd groom off your arms
if i were i

call, response: immunity's hope

                    nurture my future
        on clock's other hand
mother science burns father nature
        sends gender to war
            score at halftime
predicts fertile tomorrow
        staph. aureus affects primarily canadians
switch citizen for immunity's new community

c5, r2: mikado's unconscious

insistence on resistance pushes bacterial mutation
        small cell's elation at technology's defeat
                thought bunnies were bad?
we reproduce on your juice
        the yum yum of intestinal fluid
corruption of gut   cowboys of inner space
race irrelevant   we hump from meat machine to meat machine
        sweeter than salt   no halt to proliferation plus differentiation
we model minority's   retort to business
plague robber to abandon ship

c5, r3: biomechanics

or build it anew
                    meatcraft a charming host
to the meekest of sheep   micro trumps velcro
the grow-op's co-op   taters for later
            alma mater   matters less than bodies
        everybody needs some
as substrate for the ingrate
        the cheese in your please
begging desire to release the ad man

c5, r4: media coverage

mikado's bravado   babytalks asian child
      gone wild as girls   flashing headlights in media hailstorm
        worm in the brain confronts executioner   cellphone camera
captures undignified taunts   haunt of victorian heights
othering orient to vent repression   held in wolds and shires
       geography's mire racing animal to man
the can can of kitschy kitschy ya ya

c5, r5: reading strategy

irony bored by the boat of quotes
        shirt flaps for body

                        homuncular as junk
dna   scrabble for meaning   leaning to triple word score
              whores' representation of real thing
cola's pepto dismal
        a sign of the times
                    new roman

circle, square: precedence

empire of the fences   species barrier rights don't cross
     science swims daily   seeking surplus equipment
air forced from outer to inner space   trace of taint
paint needed to whitewash powergrab   memsahib's
passage from india
     splendid blender of trading co.s east india, hudson's bay
        tribute of my tributaries
veinous and heinous
     infecting earth, infecting body of cousin other
punish likeness
     wait for broken mirror to spike back

c6, s2: mutation's revenge

or reflect junk broken free to manifest ancient traits
        platelets and hemoglobin
stroking for another animal
           everything old is a new gain
       in the chain of eve's volition
adam's contrition   conditions for unexpected mutation
      cousin's elation   mesopotamian basin renewing after flood
      of human-induced disease
          brewing a new stew
bitchy as simian kitchen
      itchin' for a fresh kind of finger lickin'
finally stickin' it to the man

c6, s3: ooo ooo eee eee

oh brother artful art thou
      seeking the how of our connection
only to understand yourself   shelf shakespeared not stirred
          by the alternate whirr   the in of intelligence
the sin in the pardon
          my eden unbroken by the word made fodder
for reason's treason   telltale heart beating in surrogate body
      your innocent double   frank-n-furtive
as pocky's horror   the girl in the picture hearts
        a fixture in the self-construction
      of man made ham

c6, s4: got cells?

ha ha
                    poke's on you   tidy insertion
take another little piece of my heart
                              part stands in hole
          simian metonym swings hymn of hope
fresh hiss of cousin blood in corroded veins
          skein of immunosuppressants   unpleasant necessity
of social avoidance
                         in case of contact with mad cow know how
               kowtow in the go-down
          slow as a row boat from china

serenade

new cultural politics of intimacy
     i am he as you are he as you are me and we are all together
birds of a flu   fish of a feather
   pooling cellular capacity   to hybridize our chameleon
anaesthetize our chimera   mythic's specifics   documented on ebay
       relay of baby blue eyes   implant
           from sight to second   helping the sound of au délà
hum   comme çi comme   des garçons
     les filles s'habille
       couture of butchered interiors

circumference, volume: spilling lesson

look   those who didn't die
        in weightlessness   crash test   inoculation experiment
we were saved   save the chimps
        from coulston's violation of animal rights
a florida sanctuary
                chance of humankindness
        recognizes arc from animal to cultural
                        reconstruct community in the absence of wild
imagining africa and in what part of their being
                buzzing through these new world fields and swamps
second nature improves incarceration
                        waiting for the call of the filed

c7, v2: the hum of ham

cat's out of cradle
    treadle spins civilization
                porous chorus springs mutation selection
finch chimp fish or him
    predilection for reproduction   seduction of expansion coefficient
                twinkling flesh things and green things
      cell's bells call in greed's bills
cashing out on a may day morning

auto matter

yut

we're occupied by degrees
houses call to us
in their variety
and sameness
breezy terrace, diocesan boys' school
blackwood place, malka drive
the apartment above the bus terminal in kowloon

movement accelerates
addresses accumulate
we think our possessions afford us memory
protractor set
ceramic monkey from red rose tea box
black acrylic sweater
white hearts circle shoulders following fair isle design

these matter the way
memory matters
shattered in transit
we eye airplanes hopefully
the "never forget" of what can't be retrieved

yee

photographs accumulate
unmarked in cardboard boxes
steps crumble concrete
in pale sun
nam hoi paddies point to
old hakka village
trampled by race horses
bellilios girls' school
london school of economics
harrowsmith magazine wheat germ fringes brewer's yeast

heritage squashes
she cultivates turnip greens dreaming of choy sum
i fetishize beaded belts and leather tooling
seek my own face
in books that say the ones here before
have vanished
(2008 shirley laughs: *not dead—hiding*)
town vs outport
hope of may '68 taunts cultural revolution
headless bodies drift into fragrant harbour

her smile strains beneath weight
at two wendy ferals fierce
i retreat to animal kingdom
to switch species might mean escape

sam

who began the rumour
occupying forces used diocesan as execution ground?
administration switches boys' school to japanese military hospital
possibility of buried patients
grounds ghosts biopolitical
identification unknown

dad remembers sweets
from the harryleilas
burfi, gulabjamen, jelebi
friend colonial connection
"civilizing" our difference in dainty kindness

loyal teacher smuggles food to british forces
interned at sham shui po
winnipeg grenadiers prophecy
future haven
from bad fortune (red guards overrun)
or good (extreme capital accumulation)

say

haven is relative
"god's her own father
and she don't even believe in 'im"
our lady of lourdes
romances *another place, not here*

mm

gin drinker's line stretches eleven miles
faces japanese forces: 38th division of 23rd army
three regiments of infantry
the 38th mountain artillery regiment
38th engineering regiment
two independent mountain artillery regiments
two anti-tank gun battalions
a mortar battalion
another engineering regiment
three transport regiments
and two river crossing companies

the gin drinkers fold

back to royal rifles and rajputs
winnipeg grenadiers, punjabs, and royal scots

articulate history
in the honourable language of war
between imperial japanese lines of attack and british colonial defence
read silence to find family

look

little hong kong
pok fu lam
aberdeen
wong nei chong gap
wanchai gap
strategic positions or subway stops

she knows the skip from bellilios to breezy terrace
winding up conduit road

tsut

bring in the fox lady
to account for the elder brother who died at five
to remember tb stigma
marking great-grandmother's departure
aha aha breathing to account for
blind second wife
pride of singsong sister
raising dead wife's children as own
fox lady sighs
fox lady sniffs
wails cantonese opera tunes on old analogue cassettes

baht

hang hang
hang hui gaai bin jup goh chaang

gow

outside the bank of china
diagonally across the street from the chater road cricket club
old security guard eyes handsome steward
thinks: *a good husband*
for my daughter

sup

hah   aha
breathe fire foxily
to stimulate organs without bodies
call to the animal part
movement begins at night
down by the water   yes
remembering salmon   hm
          the streams that were there
brewery creek
               china creek
                         31st avenue   east 18th
addresses beneath the surface
     ghosts above:
     alaska cedar   douglas fir   coast redwood   sitka spruce
          busy bacteria
                                   fix nitrogen
hah   mmmm hmmmmm

sup yut

grandfather marks decision   cross chinese line to freedom
                                                                  a journey begins

natural feet but no education
great-grandmother runs easily

                    bound feet and reading knowledge
                    great-great-aunt must be carried
                    but her three kingdoms ease our weary minds

                         one war escapes another
                 by train? by bus? desperate scramble in heat fear
the push-n-shove of crowd survival
        stirs rising tempers   how petty wearies on history's backdrop
                                            chun king shimmers unreachable

you can still live
in an occupied city
yeh yeh sells dried goods in guangzhou: lin chi and beans

            we hide   eat makeshift meagre   say her stories
                                               soothe ancestral time

sup yee

a monastery in the hills
                           buddhist swims earth religion in time with the tao
        in beat with a room   wood plank bed and straw mat
to retreat from family life

prediction sticks shake death from bamboo jar   three times for accuracy
           long hours of waiting   a kind of peace

years later we ride the bus
                hike half an hour to picnic
  a servant took us there he sd   (class difference cracks order's belonging)
in another after
                   stream floods   land slides
                              rthk reports ten students killed

sup sam

the unconscious is structured like a language
      native informs "civilized" part
all girls have eyes sd oryx
why does it matter whether i am the same person?
      oral historicizes memory
the been there
         of done that

sup say

anamnesis means the acquisition of knowledge
as the return memory lost in the shock of birth

sup mm

i repress (newfoundland)
      the way you repress (china)
seagulls screech as they circle
         over clattering tide
               pulls pebbles back to sea
grey one grey one blue one grey one brown one grey one sea glass green
                                 shoves water
polishes fish and rock
      wet·wash of my emergence

sup look

sign over door at ministry of fisheries:
in cod we trust
        currency of north atlantic
                emergency of memory
take me back to my western home

sup tsut

read body as registers switch
       fox woman arms intellectual
              green as heart grows aching for
conversation not admitted
against the raging howl of righteous men boy men
screeching look-at-me-look-at-me
now that they've glimpsed you
for the first time
and want a juicy slice

have none of it
our conversation rustles
in the adjustment of skirts

sup baht

on the musqueam reserve
by the flag shop at burrard and fourth
at bayswater and point grey road
out by jericho beach
down by the grandview superstore
          undercurrents fishy beginnings
               the upstream ladder
moves from salt water to fresh
what the city covers it also
                         remembers
      anadromous
symbiotic
   scrambling latin to find real beneath estate

sup gow

the path is overgrown and the white
girl doesn't want you to know
it's there
what you remember is
fog   an ache
in the legs   brush, bracken
how rot of woods
smells like human waste

the rusted car
      how did it get there?
even then its machine-ness
half undone
      fog rushes to return it
      to forest
here everything is wind
         and element
cold soaks both bone and frame

in the dream it's a bike and the white boy says
yes, you can enter
the memories are yours

      so you show him and rita
patches of chanterelle
carpeting the floor of memory's woods

the bike is buried to its top rims
the ocean comes sooner
and closer than you remember

between flatrock and torbay
dirt road accesses middle cove
tide clatters grey rock over grey rock over
caplin in june
spawn hopeful
of asian market

in the dream it's the malka drive bog trail
that takes you there
the cove is smaller and stiller
shed your clothes and swim

the white
boy turns it into a library
lie behind the futon
here's plato's lost text on laughter

room or
          alcove
the middle ground fills with students
waiting
for something to happen

something happened
on that cuso trip
says lily
something that brought the internment back
he lived with his mother for the rest of his life
never worked again

my middle cove balances white
girl's refusal
this is canada
god's your own father
believe   believe

against white
boy's lead
memory shows me the wrong road
or two different roads
as the same

to gather mushrooms
to rush the tide
one day the library
will reveal the middle
            word   the line to undo
            portugal cove's subdivision
return turnip greens
the yellow door
the heap of rocks harvested
to make a garden

yee sup

crazy roommate is crazy
for a reason
                  her fridge is jammed with boiled
                  spider crabs
i eat them
pull stringy flesh from inside
green tubular legs
cram my mouth with sweet
                  she washes dishes

don't go into the dining room
it's full of dust and cat fur
           there are faucets in the walls
           above the cacti and household ivy

there's an unused kitchen with gas range
plopped unloved between bedroom and bathroom

           who is julie rain bosch?
           when did she introduce us?

the unconscious is structured
like a sandwich
           syntactic mayonnaise
                  disguises indecipherable meat

yee sup yut

bound foot great-great-aunt had two daughters
        a teacher and a soldier's wife

like you
            the teacher changed jobs a lot

the soldier went to military college in guangzhou
        joined the kuomintang
        fought communists in north china

was caught and imprisoned in a well
        forged documents to grant his own release
            ran all the way back to hong kong

i saw the tattered page
stamped with a big red chop

yee sup yee

neither red nor dead
        sun yat-sen precedes general chiang
                precedes the gentle chairman not yet tainted by
a thousand flowers
        great leap backwards   glass
kneeling sessions of cultural devolution

neither reformed nor deformed
        chinese characteristics open to hog market economy
dish cantopop to race the pace of labour
in airless factory rooms

        monumentalize gorge's displacement
harness yangtze river to show america
the brilliant lights of shanghai

what we do to our rivers
we can do to your debt

forget the pain in my golden lotus feet
forget the unfinished escape
great-great-aunt ghosts: like dong zhou who killed a village of his own civilians
paraded their heads through chang' an
to pretend success in battle

                            lin chi softens slowly in mouth

yee sup sam

loyal teacher
passes colonizer
food through the gates
of his internment camp
look we ration
look we reason

when we relish "ing"

yee sup say

whatever you do
don't write about me

if the communists hadn't liberated
if the british hadn't colonized
if mccarthy hadn't scared
if the green card hadn't refused

      oh say can you see
      flying our caravan east to go west
              for work hard and earnest
         california dreamin'
              the most beautiful girl in the usa

yee sup mm

poppy induces copy
call it beginning
that part of the cycle where you choose
to start
opium roulettes british
the lease's leash
99 is one card short
of a century
suzy ditzes
her white
dress flaps ghostlike after monsoon shower

yee sup look

stop blossoming
popo's eyes know how the tall lady knows
·ballet's an escape from gung gung's derision
her jue yook bang's too salty
cheah
as he slurps it down

we're petty like this
fox lady haunts cricket grounds
sly civility mimics (life)
clutching ancestral excess
while the mainland scraps
three ways

yee sup tsut

On this, the purchase day,
the girl is to enter the ...Tong.
The household head may change
her name and treat her as a maid servant.

If on the hills or on the water,
in winter or summer,
any accident should befall [the girl]
it shall be the will of Heaven.

The widow may not pester [the purchaser]
nor can the relatives come
to his door to make accusations
[about the death].[1]

---

1.   Hayes, James. "Women and Female Children in Hong Kong and South China to 1949: Documents of Sale and Transfer." *Hong Kong: A Reader in Social History*. Oxford: OUP, 2003. 426-462.

yee sup baht

knowing when to stay soft
the wisdom of what the moment calls for

yee sup gow

forces of hystery slap our asses
to the shopping mall
shirt a dress
a rolex watch
balms fetish to calm
the open-jaw ticket

sam sup

they were two
in '41
kmt and ccp strife
while rising son's co-prosperity bayonets
comfort stations manchuria to hk
food rations and curt curfew
we defy lights out
place brown paper over bulbs
until japanese military police come knocking
chinese collaborator beside

the price: popo's pride
means body
puppet parrots until second great-uncle
declares tennis chums
rank high on collusion's tower

catch my drift?
pollution after birth
saves invader's face
shock horror resonates to current
dinner table

eat up
it's not the occupation

sam sup yut

or gung gung's racket
rumours hollow handle
a spy for chinese nationalists?
newspapers or special messages?
escapes to macao
with only half the family
popo is left behind

sam sup yee

i was so unhappy then
i'm happy now
why should i remember?
popo muses in sports shop english
queried by the querulous
in n/a's island vacuum

sam sup say

but remember the sports shop
rackets restrung with nylon or catgut
shelves of shoes
pressurized cans of balls
poured into machine
smack 'em back with a satisfying   pop!
hk country club fashions '60s swank
riding uncle's beamer to
deep water bay

forty love takes effort to arrive
at deuce
approach game and return to deuce again
and the japanese toy store next door
hello
                hello kitty

sam sup mm

in relation to soldiers
body of my grandmother
chinese women had
in brutal bodies as child, husband witness
continues hong kong nanjing manchuria

in relation to tourists
great-uncle's sport shop fortune
fascinates clubs and racquets
chinese recreates tennis whites

in relation to american passport
eh bomb
disposable's likeness
shadows sidewalk and radiation
peel of skin   kin
returns mushrooms
to cloud our soup

in relation to friendship
can
          asian
springs through looking glass

to say "japanese"
registers fox levels
address redress
as fortune turns id
on difference's wheel of same

sam sup look

2009 dioscesan old boys
gather round the table
wax nostalgic
as moon wanes above smog
sushi in TO's cabbagetown
and coffee at lettieri
        outside the glass
        young private school boys
        in brass-buttoned blue blazers
        hair black as once
        descend from tour bus
        mimic civility
        sly lovely
        hang seng rattles
other indexes

sam sup tsut

indecent indices suggest
it was that way too
both lands either/or
the score at airport lounge
twists revolution's hope against cap's scope
we float our "i"
right between the eyebrows
        third pace
                laughs out both sides of mouth
tears damned as yangtze river
        floods mud people anew
displace me again
                          sam

sam sup baht

fox lady begins the end
        aha   fix four quarters in armature
drive into machine
           to restart cycle

it's a dirty topic   canadian studies student muses
        aching for universal
screwdriver
          you're reading too much into it

seek source of stream on musqueam reserve
        thank that which has not been buried
                    eat salmonberries
        as shallow water trips over rocks
step twice into the same memory
           structure gushing
no anchor wolf
          no anchor word
no anchor wow
        no anchor way
tao takes a bow
hum homme ham womb om
       sum lob femme loom comb
rem dome
     plumb foam
          trim scam man grub bone

mmmmm hmmmmm
               home

Acknowledgements

Thank you: Rita Wong, for teaching me so much about movement in language and in life, and for a great ninth-hour read; Roy Miki, for friendship, wisdom, and damn good ideas; Hiromi Goto, steadiest of friends from outer to inner space.

For fabulous editorial support, and for encouragement, enthusiasm, half-bred eyes and slanted ears, a big thank you to Fred Wah. This is where the "i" went.

Thank you because you get me, let me say pretty much anything about writing or life, and continue to like me anyway: Shirley Bear, Pauline Butling, Slavia Miki, David Khang, David Chariandy.

Thank you to Aruna Srivastava and Ashok Mathur for friendship and an open home in Mountain Standard Time. Thank you to the Calgary "kids," a.k.a. Janet Neigh, Frances Kruk, Nikki Reimer, Jason Christie, derek beaulieu, Chris Ewart, Sandy Lam, Travis Murphy, Nikki Sheppy, Natalie Walschotts, and Christian Bök; and to the Banff "hobbits," especially Myron Campbell, and hobbit wranglers Michael Boyce and Sandra Dametto.

Thank you to Nadine Chambers for sharing her island home in the last days of this project.

"Rachel" is based on the Ridley Scott film *Blade Runner* and Philip K. Dick's novel *Do Androids Dream of Electric Sheep?* I am grateful to them.

The earliest versions of "Rachel" and "nascent fashion" were self-published through True Lai's Chapbook Press as handmade chapbooks in editions of twenty-four.

Much appreciation to Michael Barnholden, Glen Lowry, and *West Coast LINE* for their enthusiasm about these poems and for publishing, in whole or in part, "Rachel," "nascent fashion," and "ham." Thanks especially, Mike, for the reprints of "Rachel" in chapbook form.

Thank you to Ryan Fitzpatrick and MODL Press, for a second chapbook version of "nascent fashion."

"auto matter" borrows many words, including short phrases from of Dionne Brand's In Another Place, Not Here and Margaret Atwood's Oryx and Crake.

Thank you to the Writer-in-Residence Program in the English Department at Simon Fraser University and its organizers: Roy Miki, Jeff Derksen, Steve Collis, David Chariandy, and especially Sophie McCall.

Many thanks to my immediate family: Yuen-Ting Lai, Tyrone Lai, and Wendy Lai for your support, love, stories, and corrections, which grew and fed "auto matter." Thank you also to my dear aunt Yuen-Fong Woon for sharing her memoir and lots of memories too. I have drawn on her memoir for parts of "auto matter." Big thanks to my maternal grandmother Tsui-Pun Wai-Chee for her love, stories, and belief in me.

Many thanks to Brian Lam and Robert Ballantyne of Arsenal Pulp Press for their professionalism and faith in my work, in this project as in many past. Thank you to Susan Safyan for editorial logistics. Thank you to Shyla Seller for the wonderful design.

Last but not beast, thank you to Edward Parker for love, patience, meows, and clean plates. Sorry about the bunched-up dishtowel.

A note about transliterations: I have not transliterated Cantonese words and sounds according to any one particular system, although I am aware of several systems of standardization: Meyer–Wempe, Yale, and Lau, as well as, more recently, Jyutping and Penkyamp. (If I had wanted authenticity, accuracy, or just a different feel, I could have used traditional or simplified Chinese characters, but I chose not to.) Rather, I transliterated here with conscious whimsy, recalling the way I transliterated as a child. Where I recalled more than one spelling, I chose those with the greatest possibilities for resonance in English (in the spirit of Zukofsky's translations) as a way of adding to the sound play carried on throughout this book. The resonance of spelling, in other words, is intentional.

rachel thanks:

ridley scott, philip k. dick, sigmund freud, donna haraway, angela rawlings, pyotr ilyich tchaikovsky, e.t.a. hoffmann, william shakespeare, herman hupfeld, sianne ngai, robert browning, luce irigaray, blondie, david bowie

with varying degrees of gratitude ham acknowledges:

max raabe, britney spears, the beatles, homi bhabha, david bowie, emily brontë, colonel sanders, elizabeth barrett browning, bryan adams, nim chimpsky, the coen brothers, the coulston foundation, miles davis, charles darwin, e.m. forster, susan aglukark, jean-paul gaultier, gilbert and sullivan, glico, god, jane goodall, donna haraway, the everly brothers, jam ismail, janis joplin, koko, frances kruk, merchant ivory, peter schilling, patty labelle, audre lorde, nasa, oscar mayer, gene roddenberry, j.m. schneider, jamie uys, william shakespeare, u2, sophocles, neal stephenson, kurt vonnegut, elton john, cornel west, rita wong

countless others, i'm sure—accidental and oriental

photograph by Edward Parker

Larissa Lai is the author of the novels *When Fox is a Thousand* (Press Gang, 1995; Arsenal Pulp, 2004) and *Salt Fish Girl* (Thomas Allen, 2002). She has published several chapbooks, most notably *Eggs in the Basement* (Nomados, 2009), and is co-author (with Rita Wong) of the poetry book *sybil unrest* (Line Books, 2009). Born in La Jolla, California, Lai grew up in St. John's, NF, and recently relocated from Vancouver to Calgary, where she is an Associate Professor in the English department at the University of Calgary. She holds a PhD in English from the University of Calgary and an MA in Creative Writing from the University of East Anglia, UK.